Ash Wednesday to Easter

A *Daily Journey*

Barry J. Trick

D1275091

Paulist Press
New York / Mahwah, NJ

Cover image by Michael Ninger / Shutterstock.com
Cover design Sharyn Banks
Book design Lynn Else

Library of Congress Cataloging-in-Publication Data

Trick, Barry J.
    Ash Wednesday to Easter : a daily journey / Barry J. Trick.
    p. cm.
    Includes bibliographical references.
    ISBN 978-0-8091-4813-4 (alk. paper) — ISBN 978-1-58768-095-3
1. Lent—Prayers and devotions. 2. Easter—Prayers and devotions.
I. Title.
    BV85.T65 2012
    242'.34—dc23

                                            2012039356

Published by Paulist Press
997 Macarthur Boulevard
Mahwah, New Jersey 07430

www.paulistpress.com

Printed and bound in the
United States of America

Contents

To My Mother
Roberta Elizabeth Trick
Who Daily in Word and Action
Taught Her Nine Sons
The Value of Faith and Love and Family

Introduction

Every successful journey begins with a clear destination and the determination to overcome all the obstacles and challenges along the way. Our Lenten journey to Easter is no exception.

Our loving Savior himself spent forty days in prayer and fasting and sacrifice. Jesus was preparing himself for his greatest sacrifice, his most magnanimous act of love. "No one has greater love than this, to lay down one's life for one's friends" (John 15:13). Christ's journey to Jerusalem and to resurrection is our own journey to Easter and to a deeper sharing in the life and grace of our risen Savior. There is, however, a dramatic difference. While Jesus walked alone through the bitterest hours of his painful journey, he now walks with us on our way to Easter. Each day he fills and renews our hearts with his love. Each day he guides our minds through the darker moments. With his sure grace, each day he strengthens us in our weaker moments. The day after Easter, Jesus walked to Emmaus with two disciples. Finally recognizing their Lord, they said, "Were not our hearts burning within us while he was talking to us on the road, while he was opening the scriptures to us?" (Luke 24:32). Today it is on our journey to Easter that Christ walks with us—our model, our strength, our very life.

We associate "sacrifice" with the Lenten journey. Isn't sacrifice important in every relationship? To show us his boundless love, Christ Jesus "emptied himself, taking the form of a slave" (Phil 2:7). On Calvary he completed his perfect sacrifice in his greatest act of love for us. "And I, when I am lifted up from the earth, will draw all people to myself" (John 12:32). In its roots the word *sacrifice* is a positive, not a negative, word. The Latin *sacra facere* (sacrifice) means to make something holy, to give it a value greater than it had in itself. Whatever we give or share in love is made holy by that gift and by our love. The money given to alleviate another person's suffering is made holy by that giving. The efforts made to reconcile the hurt or the angry are also holy. The time taken to strengthen a relationship with a spouse or with one's children is definitely holy. The simpler, more frugal meal prepared so that others might simply eat reflects Christ's own spirit and sacrifices. Each of these requires some giving or some giving up, and that sacrifice makes the gift and the giver more holy, more like—and more alive in—the risen Christ. St. Irenaeus wrote, "The glory of God is a person fully alive."[1] Is that not the destination of our journey to Easter?

The forty days of Lent provide us with a unique opportunity to move closer to Christ Jesus, whose arms and heart are open to us each step of our journey. Each day's opportunities can be taken or lost. For the resolute Christian, strengthened by grace, each opportunity is resolution and determination acted upon. Each day of our Lenten journey we can use that day's opportunities to know Christ more fully, to love him more deeply, to follow him more surely. Our journey is not to Good Friday, but to his Easter and our own new life. At the end of the Lenten journey we want to be able to say with St. Paul, "It is no longer I who live, but it is Christ who lives in me" (Gal 2:20). At the end of forty days we want to celebrate our risen Christ and our own renewed life in him:

> His wounds are now healed
> And Jesu sings his Resurrection
> In my waking, beating heart.[2]

How to Use This Book

In prayer we open our hearts and speak to a loving God who knows and listens to our voice. In prayer God speaks to us, as our Lord and guide, as our loving parent. He asks that we listen as well and learn to recognize his voice. This book has been designed to foster daily prayer on our journey to Easter—and beyond. Since God gave us his revealed Word so that he could speak to us as often as we would read or listen, there is a short scriptural passage for each day of our Lenten journey. Some days that reading alone, along with the thoughts and feelings it inspires, might be a wonderful prayer. Some days that reading from scripture—and a quiet, listening heart—could draw us closer to the God who holds us in his sustaining love. Then there are other days, when we wonder if we are deaf or if God has anything to say to us at all. Every relationship has those days. That is why each scriptural passage is followed by a reflection that might open the heart to personal prayer or open the soul to helpful thought. There is not just one perfect prayer. Samuel's prayer was pleasing to God when he simply said, "Speak, Lord, for your servant is listening" (1 Sam 3:9). Mary's prayer was simple but perfect when she said, "Here am I, the servant of the Lord; let it be with me according to your word" (Luke 1:38). And yet, how equally beautifully she was praying each time she stopped and listened to her child in Nazareth or spoke from her heart to her son at Cana at the wedding feast or looked into her son's eyes on Calvary. Each time she was deepening her relationship with the Lord and center of her life. Each time she spoke from her heart and listened with patient openness there was a continuing and deepening communication that is the nourishment of every relationship. Fostering that same communication—that same patient listening, that same speaking from the mind and heart—is the main objective of this book. Strengthened by grace and sustained by daily prayer, we can journey with "our hearts burning within us" to our Savior's resurrection and our own renewed life in him (Luke 24:32).

Ash Wednesday
to Saturday

Ash Wednesday

Trust in the LORD forever, for in the LORD GOD you have an everlasting rock. For he has brought low the inhabitants of the height; the lofty city he lays low. He lays it low to the ground, casts it to the dust. The foot tramples it, the feet of the poor, the steps of the needy. The way of the righteous is level; O Just One, you make smooth the path of the righteous. In the path of your judgments, O LORD, we wait for you; your name and your renown are the soul's desire.

Isaiah 26:4–8

Christ Jesus, our Healer,

Years ago a newly published novel rocketed to the best seller lists and remained there for months and months. The film version attracted long lines of eager fans. The defining line of this amazing work was perhaps the most surprising and absurd line ever written. In this popular romance, one character insists that loving someone means never having to say you're sorry. It is precisely because we love and care about another person that, when we fail or hurt them, we must not only express our sorrow in words, but demonstrate it in our actions. Because of our frailty, or our self-absorption or willfulness, we are far from faultless. Our sins and our failings weaken, not just ourselves, but also the relationships that we value most. And you, Lord, "our soul's desire," call us not to condemnation, but to contrition, to reparation, to forgiveness, and to wholeness.

In you we find our healer and our health. In you we find the grace and strength to repair what we have damaged by our sins and failings. In you we find the loving Savior who wills only to create in us living and loving hearts. Lord, on our journey to Easter make our path to you sure and smooth. Make our steps toward you determined and certain. Amen.

Thursday after Ash Wednesday

Put away from you crooked speech, and put devious talk far from you. Let your eyes look directly forward, and your gaze be straight before you. Keep straight the path of your feet, and all your ways will be sure. Do not swerve to the right or to the left; turn your foot away from evil.

Proverbs 4:24–27

Christ Jesus,

You are the Word that existed in the beginning, the perfect expression of divine truth and love. How then could we use the words of our mouths to deceive, to hurt, to tear down, or to destroy? Lord, you have made us in your own image and likeness; help us to reflect more clearly that image in all our words and actions of this day. Keep our eyes and minds and hearts focused on you, who are our way, our truth, and our life. Lord, source of truth and perfect expression of the Father's love, help us to speak only to heal, only to enlighten and inspire, only to brighten and dispel sorrow, only to console, only to build up, only to reflect your own love in our hearts. By your grace divine, live in our hearts and minds, dispel the darkness around us with our own voices and hearts and hands. Amen.

Friday after
Ash Wednesday

For you were called to freedom, brothers and sisters; only do not use your freedom as an opportunity for self-indulgence, but through love become slaves to one another. For the whole law is summed up in a single commandment, "You shall love your neighbor as yourself."

Galatians 5:13–14

Lord and loving Father,

Our deepest yearnings are to be free—free at last from greed and needless anxiety, from self-centeredness and from self-doubt, free from hostility and bitterness, free from hatred and from all the base feelings and failings that enslave and confine us. How beautiful are the lives of all the men and women who were freed from fear and confusion by their faith in you. How beautiful the words and works of those freed from superficiality by their love for and dedication to you. How beautiful the joy and peace of those freed from confusion and anxiety by their trust in you. The freedom from want of poor Francis of Assisi. The freedom from despair of Mother Teresa. The freedom from intimidation of Sir Thomas More and Dr. Martin Luther King. Lord, help us to choose and to surrender to your love for us. Only held by your love can we know true freedom; only held in your love can we know and share true joy. Amen.

Saturday after Ash Wednesday

Let love be genuine; hate what is evil, hold fast to what is good; love one another with mutual affection; outdo one another in showing honor. Do not lag in zeal, be ardent in spirit, serve the Lord. Rejoice in hope, be patient in suffering, persevere in prayer. Contribute to the needs of the saints; extend hospitality to strangers. Bless those who persecute you; bless and do not curse them. Rejoice with those who rejoice, weep with those who weep. Live in harmony with one another; do not be haughty, but associate with the lowly; do not claim to be wiser than you are. Do not repay anyone evil for evil, but take thought for what is noble in the sight of all.

Romans 12:9–17

Christ Jesus, loving Savior,

As some of us age, we feel our capacity for sadness expand. So many sad things, so many bad things happen to so many good people. But in our darkest moments we hear your voice: "Let love be genuine; hate what is evil, hold fast to what is good." To the young, life seems so promising and dreams seem so real and so attainable. But you challenge all of us who believe to hold firm to everything that is good and to love and share with both friend and stranger. Sometimes those upon whom we rely most heavily fall short of our expectations and disappoint us. We wonder if those we love are still the same people we once knew. And again we hear your voice, "Be patient in suffering." We tire. How tired a person can get of trying to do what is right, when the results are so meager, so unrecognized. "Do not lag in zeal, be ardent in spirit, serve the Lord." Even in company, we can feel so alone, so isolated and alienated from those around us at work and even at home. What do we have in common with those who do not have the same problems or feelings or perspectives? "Rejoice with those who rejoice, weep with those who weep. Live in harmony with one another...." Lord, as we move with you toward Easter, be our strength—how can we fail? With you as our daily support, how can we fall? Amen.

First Week of Lent

Sunday

"Beware of practicing your piety before others in order to be seen by them; for then you have no reward from your Father in heaven. So whenever you give alms, do not sound a trumpet before you, as the hypocrites do in the synagogues and in the streets, so that they may be praised by others. Truly I tell you, they have received their reward. But when you give alms, do not let your left hand know what your right hand is doing, so that your alms may be done in secret; and your Father who sees in secret will reward you."

Matthew 6:1–4

Heavenly Father,

Deep within each of us is the desire to be seen, to be recognized, to be rewarded with love and praise. As a child we beamed when a smile or kind word rewarded our setting the table or cleaning our room. While you created us in your image to love, we want so much to be seen as lovable and to be rewarded with love. Only a saint like Francis of Assisi could pray, "Grant that I may seek, not so much to be loved, as to love; not so much to be understood, as to understand."[3] But how faint is the praise of others, when our quiet love and generosity can be seen and loved by you. How faint and fleeting the recognition of others, when our purer acts of kindness can be seen and loved through all the depth and height and eternity of your

11

infinite goodness. "The last temptation is the greatest trea-son: To do the right deed for the wrong reason."[4] Teach us to see and respond quietly to the simple needs around us. Teach us to be grateful for all of your countless blessings, and to show our gratitude by the way we care for and com-fort, support and smile at each person who needs to experience your loving care. We ask these things through Christ, our light and our life. Amen.

Monday

By contrast, the fruit of the Spirit is love, joy, peace, patience, kindness, generosity, faithfulness, gentleness, and self-control. There is no law against such things. And those who belong to Christ Jesus have crucified the flesh with its passions and desires. If we live by the Spirit, let us also be guided by the Spirit. Let us not become conceited, competing against one another, envying one another.

Galatians 5:22–26

Christ Jesus, loving Savior,

We tend to forget that you became so much like us that you also deeply felt the disappointments in your life. The rich young man who spoke with you and then sadly walked away. The apostle who denied you over and over. Even the fig tree that bore no fruit when it had been tended and nourished. "You will know them by their fruits," you reminded us (Matt 7:20). Nourish us with your grace, tend us in your strength, so that we may bear the fruits of the Spirit that you look for in us. When we begin to feel hostility, fill our flawed hearts with your love. When we see sadness in another, stop us from turning away. Help us share the joy of your presence in our lives. When we are tempted to break faith or trust—in our actions or even in our thoughts—strengthen us with your unfailing grace. When we start to savor excuses more than resolution, help us to remember your enduring strength through your own temptations and through your terrible sufferings. Come, Holy Spirit, healer and comforter, fill the hearts of your faithful that we may live in his grace and bear in our daily lives the fruits of his love. Amen.

Tuesday

My friends, if anyone is detected in a transgression, you who have received the Spirit should restore such a one in a spirit of gentleness. Take care that you yourselves are not tempted. Bear one another's burdens, and in this way you will fulfill the law of Christ.

Galatians 6:1–2

Christ Jesus, Source of Mercy and Forgiveness,

The gospels show you, over and over again, lifting up those who have failed or fallen, while warning all of us against self-righteousness and hardness of heart. "Let anyone among you who is without sin be the first to throw a stone at her" (John 8:7). You cautioned us against trying to get the speck out of our brother's or sister's eye, while ignoring the beam in our own. When our love for another and our love for you prompt us to correct anyone, may we always act "in a spirit of gentleness," remembering our own imperfections. How easy it is to savor a sense of superiority when correcting another; how little we are like you, our Savior, when we do the right thing for the wrong reason or in the wrong spirit. When we see frailty in another, we should be reminded of our own different but deep faults in ourselves. Only by your grace can we remain in grace, and only by bearing one another's burdens can we truly remain in your love. Amen.

Wednesday

There are six things that the LORD hates, seven that are an abomination to him: haughty eyes, a lying tongue, and hands that shed innocent blood, a heart that devises wicked plans, feet that hurry to run to evil, a lying witness who testifies falsely, and one who sows discord in a family.

Proverbs 6:16–19

Lord and loving Father,

As we turn away from our world's daily horrors, given such chilling detail by today's technology, we want, more and more, only a positive, uplifting perspective from our faith. Our emotions feel a surfeit. Enough! We want to hear some good news, think beautiful thoughts—feel good again. And the last emotion anyone wants to feel is guilt. But freedom from guilt is not freedom from pain. If there is no guilt, there is no real distinction between right and wrong, between what is pleasing to God and what is "an abomination to him," between what builds up the human family and what tears it down. The boundless forgiveness of our Father does ask something of us; it asks that we recognize and reject those things that destroy what God seeks to build up in his human family. His boundless mercy asks that we recognize and reject what is contrary to his word and will. Our loving God, who so humbly became human, asks an honest humility of us. This eternal Word who is Truth itself asks that we speak truthfully. This Savior, who shed his own blood that we might be brothers and sisters in him, asks that we empty our hearts of hostility and malice. This Redeemer, who prayed for unity the night before he died, asks that we reject discord and work daily for harmony in the family that is his mystical body. Lord, if you are our strength, then how can we fail? Amen.

Thursday

For if those who are nothing think they are something, they deceive themselves. All must test their own work; then that work, rather than their neighbor's work, will become a cause for pride. For all must carry their own loads.

Galatians 6:3–5

Lord and loving Father,

Religion exists to draw us closer to you, the source of our divine image and divine life. It does not exist to make us feel superior to others. If we could only see ourselves through others' eyes, we might have some interesting revelations. That perspective would save us from so much foolishness; it would save us from deluding ourselves. Then again, perhaps we should pray that we could see ourselves as you, Lord, see us. You look at each of us individually; you give each of us graces, as you give each of us our crosses. Why should I ever want to compare myself with another or look down on another? When I think I can boast, it is your grace working in me, drawing me closer to you and your boundless love. When I fail, it is my own frailty pretending to be strength. Lord, open my heart more fully to your love. Open my will more fully to your grace, so that in each day's struggle I may boast with St. Paul, "It is no longer I who live, but it is Christ who lives in me" (Gal 2:20). Amen.

Friday

He said, "Naked I came from my mother's womb, and naked shall I return there; the LORD gave, and the LORD has taken away; blessed be the name of the LORD."

Job 1:21

Lord and loving Father,

All that you give has been unearned and undeserved. All that you take has been yours and yours alone from the beginning. Naked we come; naked we shall return. And between this coming and this going, all that will matter is how much we have reflected that image of yourself in which we were created. What will count is not how much we possess or do not possess. Nor where we live or who we know. What will count is what we have done with each gift that you have given us, with what time you have allowed us. Martha was so anxious and troubled about so many things, so vocal in her complaints. Jesus, her friend, reminded her—only one thing is really important. Concentrate on that important thing—letting God live in your life—and the other things will be taken care of. Lord, accepting your daily gifts is so easy. Help us with the hard part—dealing with the losses and the failures of our more difficult days. Sustain us in faith, strengthen us in trust, support us in your love, so that we can end each day with the words of the psalmist: "I will sing of your steadfast love, O LORD, forever" (Psalm 89:1). Amen.

Saturday

Do not be deceived; God is not mocked, for you reap whatever you sow. If you sow to your own flesh, you will reap corruption from the flesh; but if you sow to the Spirit, you will reap eternal life from the Spirit. So let us not grow weary in doing what is right, for we will reap at harvest time, if we do not give up. So then, whenever we have an opportunity, let us work for the good of all, and especially for those of the family of faith.

Galatians 6:7–10

Lord and loving Father,

Thank you for the easy days—for the days when it is so easy to do what is right. Thank you for the times when doing good feels good, when we are energetic and enthusiastic. But, Lord, how much more often we grow tired of doing good and want to give up, or at least procrastinate. Sustain us with your strength, when doing your will is difficult. Remind us of your Son speaking to people who walked away when the words became too harsh. Remind us of your Son during his terrible agony in the garden, so tormented that his sweat became as drops of blood, so anxious that he prayed that the cup might pass away. Be with us, as you were with your own Son, so that we too might be sustained through all the difficult days and challenges. Give us, not just our daily bread, but our daily grace and strength, so that we might use every opportunity to "work for the good of all," but especially those whom you have given us to love. Amen.

Second Week of Lent

Sunday

For his eyes are upon the ways of mortals, and he sees all their steps. There is no gloom or deep darkness where evildoers may hide themselves.

Job 34:21–22

Lord and loving Father,

When we know we are being watched by someone we love or by someone we want to love us, how careful we are to let them see the good in us and in our actions. We want them to see our good side and to find us lovable, because we want and treasure their respect and love. Lord, we believe that your eyes are on us in our waking and in our sleep. But we forget. We believe that you see our every action and most private thoughts, even when we try to hide them in or with darkness. With you there is no darkness. But we forget. Whose love, more than yours, do we truly need and deeply want? Whose love is more valuable than yours? Whose love is more a source of deep happiness and comfort and unending joy? Lord, help us not to forget—that your love is eternal and boundless and beyond price, that your eyes are upon us whether we are waking or sleeping, that there is no one we want to see our good actions and our best selves more than you. Eternal Father, in whose eyes we live and move and have our being, fill us with your life and grace, so that when you look at us you may see a reflection of your Beloved Son in whom you were so well pleased. Amen.

Monday

But God, who is rich in mercy, out of the great love with which he loved us even when we were dead through our trespasses, made us alive together with Christ—by grace you have been saved—and raised us up with him and seated us with him in the heavenly places in Christ Jesus, so that in the ages to come he might show the immeasurable riches of his grace in kindness toward us in Christ Jesus.

Ephesians 2:4–7

Creator and gracious Comforter,

Death seems so final. There are even those who look for nothing beyond death. Death, darkness—nothing! And death would be final—or worse—because of our continuing betrayals and rejections of your infinite goodness. This image that you created to reflect your goodness and your own boundless happiness, we daily mar. But to our daily rejections and failings you have always responded with more mercy than anger. Boundless seems your love for us, infinite your mercy and grace. And how short-lived your anger. In our feeblest attempts to reflect your goodness, you see your Beloved Son living in us through his grace. In your Beloved Son, you were well pleased. His suffering and dying united his love for you, the Father, and his love for us, his flawed and frail brothers and sisters. In this Redeemer and in this Redeemer's grace alone we live and move and have our being. In him we are always brought to life. Through his grace we are saved. With him we will be raised up and seated in the heavenly kingdom. How immeasurable the riches of his grace. How boundless the continuing kindness of our Savior. Amen.

Tuesday

Long ago God spoke to our ancestors in many and various ways by the prophets, but in these last days he has spoken to us by a Son, whom he appointed heir of all things, through whom he also created the world. He is the reflection of God's glory and the exact imprint of God's very being, and he sustains all things by his powerful word. When he had made purification for sin, he sat down at the right hand of the Majesty on high.

Hebrews 1:1–3

Lord and loving Father,

You have spoken and you continue to speak to us in so many ways. You speak to us through the pages of scripture. You speak to us through the very words and actions of your Son when he walked among us. You speak to us in the voices around us and in the marvels of your creation. You speak to us in our own hearts and minds. But your words are lost if we are not listening. Hearing your voice in the night, Samuel awoke and gave the perfect response: "Speak, Lord, your servant is listening" (1 Sam 3:9). Lord, when you speak to us, may we too open our ears and minds and hearts to your voice. May we, like Samuel, hear you and always respond: "Speak, Lord, your servant is listening." Amen.

Wednesday

Owe no one anything, except to love one another; for the one who loves another has fulfilled the law. The commandments, "You shall not commit adultery; You shall not murder; You shall not steal; You shall not covet"; and any other commandment, are summed up in this word, "Love your neighbor as yourself." Love does no wrong to a neighbor; therefore, love is the fulfilling of the law.

Romans 13:8–10

Christ Jesus, loving Savior,

How few of us today can even name all ten of the commandments! After the first few we begin to pause, begin to repeat ourselves. How can we respect and obey what we have trouble even remembering! But you know our weaknesses even better than we do. You took on our flesh, our fatigue, our hunger, our moods, our pains. And you strengthen and simplify our lives. Love your neighbor as yourself. Do no evil to your neighbor, as you would not deliberately harm your own self. This love is the fulfillment of the law; this love is the one great commandment. Even if we perform wonders and move mountains, but have not charity, we are nothing. And to strengthen our reasons and our resolve, you have reassured us that whatever we do to even the least of our brothers and sisters, we are in fact doing to you. With your divine will so clear, what is left to us but our own choosing what is right—and your grace. Lord, in every thought and word and action, help us to choose to love our neighbor, ourselves, and you. Support us daily with your grace that we may fulfill your will and your law. Amen.

Thursday

Then Jesus told his disciples, "If any want to become my followers, let them deny themselves and take up their cross and follow me. For those who want to save their life will lose it, and those who lose their life for my sake will find it."

Matthew 16:24–25

Christ Jesus, loving Savior,

The rich young man in the gospel was not the only one to find your invitation too harsh. Ours is not a culture that likes the word *deny* when attached to the word *oneself*. Sacrifice belongs to pagan rituals, not our times. We want to *fulfill* ourselves or *find* ourselves or *look out for ourselves for a change*. We are too comfortable being Christians in name and hedonists in practice. Too often the cliché about "only going around once in this life" seems more credible than most of the maxims of the gospel. But in you, Lord, we see the expression of a pure and strong and deep love that still leaves us speechless whenever we open our hearts to you. How you denied yourself, considering your divinity not something to cling to; how you loved us so much that you chose to become one with us, like us in all things save sin. Your life among us was a daily sacrifice, ending in the horrors of that one bloody sacrifice on the cross. Why? Because you loved the Father, who loved us and willed our salvation. Because you loved us, who would never know your divine life without your loving sacrifice. You showed us and daily show us that sacrifice is love. Loving without giving oneself, without denying oneself, is a contradiction. What a beautiful invitation you have given us—to share in your own divine life and eternal happiness. Lord, fill us with your love that we may lose our frailty, our pettiness, our self-absorption and find true life in you. Amen.

Friday

For by grace you have been saved through faith, and this is not your own doing; it is the gift of God—not the result of works, so that no one may boast. For we are what he has made us, created in Christ Jesus for good works, which God prepared beforehand to be our way of life.

Ephesians 2:8–10

Father and gracious Creator,

We believe in and know how important good works are in our lives, but we are so self-focused we think mainly about the good deeds we do or should do. As important as these are, so much more awesome is your divine handiwork in our lives. How much more wonderful the gifts you have showered on us and continue to shower on us. The good things that we can do can be done only with your grace. And these simple actions are a faint expression of gratitude for your blessings to us. But the best part of what we are and do flows from your boundless love and continuing benevolence. Despite our faults and failings, you love us without comprehensible reason. We are called to return your love for reasons we could never fully list in a lifetime. How then can we boast? "Love one another as I have loved you," Jesus reminds us (John 15:12). St. Francis prayed, "Grant that I may not so much seek to be loved, as to love; not so much seek to be understood, as to understand."[5] Lord, help us love someone today, not according to the measure of what we think that person deserves, but with the gracious generosity with which you daily love us. Amen.

Saturday

Then I saw that wisdom excels folly as light excels darkness. The wise have eyes in their head, but fools walk in darkness. Yet I perceived that the same fate befalls all of them.

Ecclesiastes 2:13–14

Holy Spirit, Source of Wisdom and Inspiration,

Enlighten our minds and strengthen our hearts. The foolish person lacks good judgment or strength of will, most often both. When we are totally honest, how often do we have to admit to ourselves, "I can't believe I was such a fool"? Why do we so often choose to stumble in the darkness of our prejudices and narrow-mindedness, when we have only to look to Christ Jesus, who is our way and our truth, the surest light in this world's threatening darkness? What would Christ do? is such a simple prayer. Would he continue to nourish this resentment? Hardly. Would he be so unbending? Or unforgiving? Hardly. Would he ignore or rejoice in another person's pain? What a foolish question! Would he stumble and trip and fumble his way through difficult situations, or would he open his eyes and heart to new insights—whatever their source? The wise person has eyes because he or she tries to use the eyes of his loving Savior. Only the fool prefers to close his eyes or his mind or his heart and continue to stumble in darkness. Lord, help me shed my foolishness. Be my way and my truth and my unfailing light. Amen.

Third Week of Lent

Sunday

You must understand this, my beloved: let everyone be quick to listen, slow to speak, slow to anger; for your anger does not produce God's righteousness.

James 1:19–20

Lord and loving Father,

Often we have heard and as often ignored the old truism, "Fools rush in where angels fear to tread." Patience is a virtue. So is prudence. Why then are we so quick to speak, when we should pause and think first? Why do we so often have to act instantly and impulsively, when the situation calls for patience and clear thinking? The pace of the world around us is fast, even frenzied, often even too frenzied for our own mental and moral health. We see tempers frayed so easily, or we feel our own tempers seethe within us, ready to explode. Lord, help us to create an inner quiet in our hearts and minds, a quiet place where you dwell with your strength and peace. Remind us of St. Francis de Sales's words: "There is nothing so strong as gentleness, and nothing so gentle as real strength."[6] Lord, live within our minds and hearts today. Be our true strength and peace and gentleness. Amen.

Monday

Therefore be imitators of God, as beloved children, and live in love, as Christ loved us and gave himself up for us, a fragrant offering and sacrifice to God. But fornication and impurity of any kind, or greed, must not even be mentioned among you, as is proper among saints. Entirely out of place is obscene, silly, and vulgar talk; but instead, let there be thanksgiving.

Ephesians 5:1–4

Lord and loving Father,

What contradictory creatures we are! We celebrate the fact that you have made us in your own image, but we spend so much energy destroying or distorting each reflection of that precious image in us. Yes, God is perfect love, and we have been given life in the boundless and bountiful overflow of the divine love between Father and Son. Why then do we foster hatred and prejudice and let our antipathies fester? Fully and lovingly Christ gave himself up for us, because he was the Beloved, the only one fully pleasing to the Father. But we, baptized into his very life, fully alive through the grace of this Beloved Son, squander our energies and actions in greediness or immaturities or puerile obscenities or worse. Christ lived among us so that we would know how to live our own daily lives. Christ spoke simply and clearly so that we would have a light to guide our own thinking and a truth to inspire our every action. Lord, we are truly grateful. Help us show our gratitude by the way we reflect your own image in our words and actions of this day. Amen.

Tuesday

Very truly, I tell you, unless a grain of wheat falls into the earth and dies, it remains just a single grain; but if it dies, it bears much fruit. Those who love their life lose it, and those who hate their life in this world will keep it for eternal life. Whoever serves me must follow me, and where I am, there will my servant be also. Whoever serves me, the Father will honor.

John 12:24–26

Christ Jesus, loving Lord,

How strange, how paradoxical, the good news of your gospel sounds to our ears. We are part of a culture that celebrates self-fulfillment, self-satisfaction, self-absorption. Self-denial and sacrifice sound unwise and negative at best, damaging to one's self at the worst. But true love celebrates and takes all joy in the "other." Over and over again you showed us how much you loved us: creating us in your own image, passing over our chronic failings to redeem and uplift us, becoming one with our humanity so that we might become one with your divine Father, sharing with us your own body and blood so that we might be nourished and ennobled in our daily lives. In you we see the true meaning of sacrifice—not denial, but a making holy by giving and sharing with someone who calls us out of our limited and confined selves. Help us to expand our lives and our selves in loving. Help us to love one another as you have loved us, so that we might have life, a richer, fuller, shared life in you who are love itself. Amen.

Wednesday

But be doers of the word, and not merely hearers who deceive themselves. For if any are hearers of the word and not doers, they are like those who look at themselves in a mirror; for they look at themselves and, on going away, immediately forget what they were like. But those who look into the perfect law, the law of liberty, and persevere, being not hearers who forget but doers who act—they will be blessed in their doing.

James 1:22–25

Dear Lord and loving Father,

If religion were primarily words, eloquent and moving words, how few unbelievers there would be! If religion were primarily feelings, beautiful and poignant feelings, the world would be filled with Christians. But religion is a relationship with a loving and perfect God. Like every personal relationship, it demands a response from both sides. Like every personal relationship, it requires work, ongoing work and continuing response. Not everyone who merely "says 'Lord, Lord' will enter the kingdom of heaven" (Matt 7:21). Even Shakespeare's villainous King Claudius knew, "Words without thoughts never to heaven go."[7] Lord, give me the grace today to respond to your words I say I believe. Give me the courage to respond to the Word who took flesh and gave us all an example of how to live. You have told me that whatever I do to even the least of my brothers and sisters, I am doing to you. Lord, I believe. Help me to act on that belief in all my words and actions of this day. Amen.

Thursday

Now is the judgment of this world; now the ruler of this world will be driven out. And I, when I am lifted up from the earth, will draw all people to myself." He said this to indicate the kind of death he was to die.

John 12:31–33

Christ Jesus,

Your whole life was a preparation for your dying for our sins, for your dying to overcome both sin and death. Now you have called us to die to sin, to reject everything that diminishes your life in us. Now you call us to push from our minds all pettiness, all prejudice, all narrow-mindedness—all that diminishes your light and power. The evil in this world will be driven out, will be at least weakened a little, if I push from my own heart today all feelings of hostility, all bitterness, all self-centeredness, all arrogance. How much easier to be lifted up with and into the arms of a loving Savior, when we have shaken from our minds and hearts all the burdens of our pettiness and sins. Lord Jesus, lifted up in agony for my sins, touch my heart so that I may respond to your grace and turn away from whatever keeps me from your embrace. Amen.

Friday

What good is it, my brothers and sisters, if you say you have faith but do not have works? Can faith save you? If a brother or sister is naked and lacks daily food, and one of you says to them, "Go in peace; keep warm and eat your fill," and yet you do not supply their bodily needs, what is the good of that? So faith by itself, if it has no works, is dead.

James 2:14–17

Lord Jesus, loving Savior,

How long would we remain friends with a person who was kind and caring to us only in words, but never in actions? Not very long. But how often do we make resolutions to respond to someone in need, only to conveniently forget those good resolutions after those feelings have passed? Faith without good works is like words without actions—breath, nothing more. Good wishes, good intentions: both are so shallow if there is no follow-through. How shallow too the faith, if it is only faith enough to sustain feelings and words. Lord, so deepen our faith in you that we may show you our love today in all that we do for those you have given us to love. We ask this grace through Christ, our Lord. Amen.

Saturday

For this reason I bow my knees before the Father, from whom every family in heaven and on earth takes its name. I pray that, according to the riches of his glory, he may grant that you may be strengthened in your inner being with power through his Spirit, and that Christ may dwell in your hearts through faith, as you are being rooted and grounded in love. I pray that you may have the power to comprehend, with all the saints, what is the breadth and length and height and depth, and to know the love of Christ that surpasses knowledge, so that you may be filled with all the fullness of God.

Ephesians 3:14–19

Lord Jesus, our Light and Life,

Sometimes, like Mary Magdalene in the garden near the tomb, we are frustrated in our search for our God. Our lives can feel so wrenched and disoriented. Sometimes we feel so alienated, and so empty and so needy. And just like Mary Magdalene that Easter morning, our only problem is that we do not recognize the loving Savior standing right in front of us. Lord Jesus, all you had to do was gently speak her name, Mary, and she recognized you and all the love in your voice. Lord, you sustain me moment to moment every day of my life. All of your actions throughout your life on this earth and all of your actions now in my own life reveal "the breadth and length and height and depth" of your loving care for me. Too often, like Mary Magdalene, I don't even recognize you. Lord Jesus, open my eyes and strengthen my frail faith so that I can see you more clearly, so that I may recognize a reflection of your own love in those right before me. Lord, let me hear your voice each time you speak my name, so that, like Mary, I may see that you are with me every moment and loving me more than I will ever understand. Amen.

Fourth Week of Lent

Sunday

I have seen their ways, but I will heal them; I will lead them and repay them with comfort, creating for their mourners the fruit of the lips. Peace, peace, to the far and the near, says the LORD; and I will heal them.

Isaiah 57:18–19

Lord and loving Father,

Sometimes we are so in need of your healing that we think it is only someone else who needs the divine healer. Lord, you see our ways and our willfulness more clearly than we ourselves. It is so easy for us to fool ourselves, to see the needs and faults and shortcomings of others, while remaining so blind to our own. It was the Pharisee who prayed, thanking his God that he was not like other people. Yet more than anyone in the temple, his prayer was hollow and his soul spiritually anemic. Lord, we open our hearts and lives to your healing mercy and to your truth. Help us to see ourselves more honestly and to reflect your loving-kindness more resolutely. More honest about the depth of our need for you, our hearts will be more at peace, for in you alone do we find healing and fulfillment and peace. Amen.

Monday

And I said: "Woe is me! I am lost, for I am a man of unclean lips, and I live among a people of unclean lips; yet my eyes have seen the King, the LORD of hosts!" Then one of the seraphs flew to me, holding a live coal that had been taken from the altar with a pair of tongs. The seraph touched my mouth with it and said: "Now that this has touched your lips, your guilt has departed and your sin is blotted out."

Isaiah 6:5–7

Father and Lord of Mercy,

There is no stronger, surer theme in both the Old and New Testaments than your infinite patience and mercy in forgiving our sins. May your boundless mercy never make us casual about our failings. Not with a burning ember, but with your intense love purify our hearts of all hostility and our lips of all foul or mean-spirited words. We glory in your sustained loving and in the hope that dispels all darkness and despair and discouragement from our lives. All that you do and continue to do for us gives us more and more compelling reasons to turn away from our failings and to love you each day as you deserve to be loved. Amen.

Tuesday

Who is wise and understanding among you? Show by your good life that your works are done with gentleness born of wisdom. But if you have bitter envy and selfish ambition in your hearts, do not be boastful and false to the truth. Such wisdom does not come down from above, but is earthy, unspiritual, devilish. For where there is envy and selfish ambition, there will also be disorder and wickedness of every kind. But the wisdom from above is first pure, then peaceable, gentle, willing to yield, full of mercy and good fruits, without a trace of partiality or hypocrisy.

James 3:13–17

Christ Jesus, loving Savior,

You created this world and its wonders. You became one with us, showing us how to live in this world. Again and again, you cautioned us that your kingdom was not of this world, that your ways were not the ways of this world. The little child, the selfless widow, the contrite adulterer, the sinner so eager to see his Savior that he climbed a tree, the courageous teenager who heard the voice of an angel and said yes to the will of her God—these are the models you have given us so that we do not blindly follow those who live only in and for this world. And you sent your Holy Spirit to make us wise enough to work for peace and for justice, to show mercy and gentleness and patience, even when they are not always merited. Lord, make us strong enough, in faith and will, to do some "foolish things" each day for your sake. Amen.

Wednesday

Come now, let us argue it out, says the LORD: though your sins are like scarlet, they shall be like snow; though they are red like crimson, they shall become like wool. If you are willing and obedient, you shall eat the good of the land.

Isaiah 1:18–19

Lord and loving Father,

The poet T. S. Eliot's character Prufrock wasted his life in "a hundred indecisions" and in "decisions and revisions which a minute will reverse."[8] Lord, your prophet Isaiah reminds us that you ask of us much more strength of will and faith. "Come *now*," insists Isaiah. Procrastination is for those who wish to follow their God only in name. Excuses are for the weak or insincere. "Come *now*" because the Lord our God is infinitely good—and boundless in his mercy. Even our sins as crimson as blood, even our sins as scarlet as hatred, will be made white as snow when we change our hearts, when we empty our hearts, when we open our hearts to your love and word and will. The old saying, "Not to decide, is to decide," sounds like Prufrock's paralysis. Real love requires decisions, faith requires decisions, maturity requires decisions, you our Lord God require a decision and strength of will each time you say, "Come *now*." Lord, give us the strength each day to answer your call. Amen.

Thursday

If we say that we have fellowship with him while we are walking in darkness, we lie and do not do what is true; but if we walk in the light as he himself is in the light, we have fellowship with one another, and the blood of Jesus his Son cleanses us from all sin. If we say that we have no sin, we deceive ourselves, and the truth is not in us. If we confess our sins, he who is faithful and just will forgive us our sins and cleanse us from all unrighteousness.

1 John 1:6–9

Christ Jesus, our Way and our Truth,

So many clever writers from Voltaire to Shaw have effectively satirized the religious hypocrite—the one who feigns self-righteous holiness, the one who enjoys looking condescendingly on anyone who does not measure up to his own self-image. When you were crucified, Lord, "darkness came over the whole land" (Luke 23:44). How much was that darkness physical and how much was it our own blindness to what you were really trying to show us, and blindness to how much you wanted us to change our hearts and thinking. When we walk in the light, "we have fellowship with one another"—not envy, not contempt, not condescension, not hatred, not indifference. Fellowship. Your dying wish was that we all may be one, as you are one with the Father. When we settle for whatever is less than that, "we deceive ourselves, and the truth is not in us." The most astounding mystery, Lord, is not the incarnation, your becoming fully human. It is your miracle of letting us become one with you, reborn in your divine life. But we are alive in you only as a part of your mystical body. One with you, who are one with the Father, bonded and bound together with the love of the Holy Spirit. Fellowship. For we are a fellowship of sinners, cleansed and renewed only when "we confess our sins" and celebrate with your brothers and sisters your boundless and merciful love. Amen.

Friday

I therefore, the prisoner in the Lord, beg you to lead a life worthy of the calling to which you have been called, with all humility and gentleness, with patience, bearing with one another in love, making every effort to maintain the unity of the Spirit in the bond of peace. There is one body and one Spirit, just as you were called to the one hope of your calling, one Lord, one faith, one baptism, one God and Father of all, who is above all and through all and in all.

Ephesians 4:1–6

Lord and loving Father,

You have created each of us as an individual, and yet we are all made in your own image. We have been called to be one with you—"one body and one Spirit"—yet we love our individuality and celebrate diversity. We believe in "one Lord, one faith, one baptism," but what an astounding range of rich and diverse gifts you have given to us, your children. Who can even begin to understand the breadth and width and depth of your divine goodness, how complex and infinite the manifestations of your perfections. Lord, you ask not conformity and uniformity of us, but a full and loving use of your gifts and graces, as each of us struggles to work out your will for us "with all humility and gentleness" and patience. Amen.

Saturday

So then, putting away falsehood, let all of us speak the truth to our neighbors, for we are members of one another. Be angry but do not sin; do not let the sun go down on your anger.

Ephesians 4:25–26

Christ Jesus, loving Savior,

Even you felt irritation, aggravation, and outright anger. Exasperated with Peter's limited vision, you rebuked him with "Get behind me, Satan!" (Mark 8:33). In the temple you made a whip of cords to drive out those who were desecrating your house of prayer. For trifles, as well as for weighty reasons, we too often explode with anger or let irritations fester. Your disciple Paul gives us three helpful suggestions. First: "Speak the truth." Too often we are not even honest with ourselves. That is the starting point; how often our impatience and anger are misdirected because we are not completely honest with either ourselves or with those around us. Second: "Be angry but do not sin." Feeling angry is one thing; checking that anger quickly before we do anything hurtful is the real virtue that we have to practice, the grace that we have to pray for. Third: "Do not let the sun go down on your anger." Lord, the heart that seethes with anger too easily hardens. Even if the words "I'm sorry" are too difficult, there are other ways to speak a healing truth: "Even though I feel so angry, I want you to know that I love you, and I don't want to be angry." Lord, be our strength, our peace, and our way in moments of calm, but especially when we are angry and most in need of you. Amen.

Fifth Week of Lent

Sunday

Be careful then how you live, not as unwise people but as wise, making the most of the time, because the days are evil. So do not be foolish, but understand what the will of the Lord is. Do not get drunk with wine, for that is debauchery; but be filled with the Spirit, as you sing psalms and hymns and spiritual songs among yourselves, singing and making melody to the Lord in your hearts, giving thanks to God the Father at all times and for everything in the name of our Lord Jesus Christ.

Ephesians 5:15–20

Christ Jesus, loving Savior,

"Because the days are evil" we slip too easily and too quickly into what "everyone else" is doing. "Because the days are evil" we feel we have an excuse for compromising our more and more flexible principles. "Because the days are evil" we tell ourselves that you certainly don't expect us to be heroic, to struggle to rise above so many who are so morally casual. But you do, Lord, because you have walked among us and have shown us the way. But you do, Lord, because you have sent your Holy Spirit to fill our minds with wiser perspectives and our hearts with courage and fortitude. But you do, Lord, because sufficient for the day and each moment of the day are your graces. And so we can live each grace-filled day, not feeling constrained and gloomy, but "singing and making melody to the Lord" in our hearts, "giving thanks to God the Father at all times always and for everything in the name of our Lord Jesus Christ." Amen.

Monday

Let no evil talk come out of your mouths, but only what is useful for building up, as there is need, so that your words may give grace to those who hear. And do not grieve the Holy Spirit of God, with which you were marked with a seal for the day of redemption.

Ephesians 4:29–30

Christ Jesus, Lord and Savior,

What effects your words had on those who heard them! Your words gave light to those lost and confused. Your words uplifted the disheartened and burdened. Your words healed the suffering and the hopeless. Your words comforted those in grief and depression. Your words helped build up where there had only been a tearing down. Your words clarified the truth where there had been distortion and deception. Your words gave praise where there had been only criticism and cynicism. Redeemed by your words and life and death, you call us to reflect that image in which you have created us. Filled with your Spirit and sealed for the day of redemption, Lord, you call us to use the marvelous gift of language as you, our Lord and Savior, have used it. Be our way, our truth, and our strength. Amen.

Tuesday

Above all, maintain constant love for one another, for love covers a multitude of sins. Be hospitable to one another without complaining. Like good stewards of the manifold grace of God, serve one another with whatever gift each of you has received.

1 Peter 4:8–10

Christ Jesus, loving Savior,

You told your apostle Peter that your followers were not to forgive their brothers and sisters seven times, but seventy times seven times. You told your apostles that much had been forgiven Mary Magdalene because she had loved much. Both points reveal so much about our own lives. Because of our own faults and frailties, we are ourselves in constant need of forgiveness. We tell you, Lord, that we are sorry, but too often our attempts at any positive change are embarrassingly feeble. And so, like Mary Magdalene, our hope lies in loving intensely and consistently and joyfully, for "love covers a multitude of sins." It is so easy to say how much we love you—or anyone. Strengthen our hearts and wills, so that, like Mary, we can show our love in all our words and actions today. Help us to be good stewards of the gifts and graces you have given to us. May we leave no healing or kind or honest word unspoken today. May we leave no just or generous action undone today. What better way to show our gratitude for your gifts than by the way we use and share them. Amen.

Wednesday

Put away from you all bitterness and wrath and anger and wrangling and slander, together with all malice, and be kind to one another, tenderhearted, forgiving one another, as God in Christ has forgiven you.

Ephesians 4:31–32

Lord and loving Father,

We know we do not always think carefully enough of what we are saying, even when we are speaking to you in the words your own Beloved Son taught us: "Forgive us our trespasses, as we forgive those who trespass against us." As we forgive? What a terrible measurement to be applied to us and our failings. We are so conscious of our own rights, so angry when we have been wronged—even slightly. Bitterness, fury, shouting, reviling the other person who has wronged us. Yes, we know what St. Paul is talking about, and we always can make excuses and defend our anger so self-righteously. But as we rely on you to be compassionate, Lord, we hear you asking us to be compassionate as well. As we desperately need your forgiveness, we soberly hear ourselves asking that you forgive us, in the same measure that we forgive those who trespass against us. Father, see in us the image of your Beloved Son and help us to see that same image in others. Amen.

Thursday

Therefore take up the whole armor of God, so that you may be able to withstand on that evil day, and having done everything, to stand firm. Stand therefore, and fasten the belt of truth around your waist, and put on the breastplate of righteousness. As shoes for your feet put on whatever will make you ready to proclaim the gospel of peace. With all of these, take the shield of faith, with which you will be able to quench all the flaming arrows of the evil one. Take the helmet of salvation, and the sword of the Spirit, which is the word of God.

Ephesians 6:13–17

Christ Jesus, Lord of Life,

When we read the good news of the gospels, we tend to remember your words and admonitions of peace: "Peace I leave with you; my peace I give to you" (John 14:27). We remember that we are to turn the other cheek when struck. But our daily lives can be so complex. Often getting through the day or through a difficult situation is like doing battle. Often what is right or worthwhile has to be fought for. Often what is dangerous and destructive has to be fought against. You knew this, Lord, and wanted us to realize this, when you also said, "I have not come to bring peace, but a sword" (Matt 10:34). A contradiction? No, just a recognition of life's complexities and challenges. As you did not shrink from the challenges in your life, Lord, you do not want us to retreat or hide when something good has to be fought for and what is destructive has to be opposed. Not for greed, not for self-aggrandizement, not for ego or pleasure, but girded with "the belt of truth" and righteousness we struggle with and in you, Lord, our strength and our salvation. Amen.

Friday

I thank my God every time I remember you, constantly praying with joy in every one of my prayers for all of you, because of your sharing in the gospel from the first day until now. I am confident of this, that the one who began a good work among you will bring it to completion by the day of Jesus Christ.

Philippians 1:3–6

Christ Jesus, Source of Life,

The gospels are truly "good news" because they call us constantly out of self-absorption and alienation into joyful sharing. Lord Jesus, you assure us that you came for one reason only—that we might have life, your divine life, and might have it more abundantly. The very life you share eternally with the Father and the Holy Spirit, you lovingly share with us. Then too you call us to share this grace-filled life joyfully and meaningfully with one another. Are we not one mystical body with one source of life and one head, one faith and one baptism? "As you, Father, are in me and I am in you, may they also be in us" (John 17:21). Like St. Paul, we should celebrate your life-giving gifts and graces—confident "that the one who began a good work" in us "will bring it to completion by the day of Jesus Christ." Amen.

Saturday

Before judgment comes, examine yourself; and at the time of scrutiny you will find forgiveness. Before falling ill, humble yourself; and when you have sinned, repent.

Sirach 18:20–21

Lord and loving Father,

We are such creatures of "If only...." If only I had done this...If only I had listened to...If only I had thought first...If only I had not.... Regret follows regret, instead of leading to wisdom. Why don't our mistakes produce insights, and why don't we learn and grow from our failings? We smile at the child who pouts and says, "I can do it myself!"—only to fail miserably. And yet we too often are equally blind to how much we rely on you, Lord, to do all the things that should be done in our own lives. Are control and patience needed? We need your help. Are wisdom and diplomacy needed? We are often too rash and impetuous; we need your help. In short, we need humility, a humility that recognizes our dependence on you. Relying on you—on your grace and on your strength—we can avoid so many falls, so many avoidable mistakes. We need enough humility to admit when we have sinned, showing true repentance and a hunger for your forgiveness. Lord, give us the grace to begin now—not later, not when we are in distress. Then it may be too late, and we will be left with nothing but our regrets. Lord, open our hearts to your grace and strength. Amen.

Holy Week

Passion/Palm Sunday

As he rode along, people kept spreading their cloaks on the road. As he was now approaching the path down from the Mount of Olives, the whole multitude of the disciples began to praise God joyfully with a loud voice for all the deeds of power that they had seen, saying, "Blessed is the king who comes in the name of the Lord! Peace in heaven, and glory in the highest heaven!"

Luke 19:36–38

Christ Jesus, loving Savior,

Shakespeare described love as "an ever-fixed mark / That looks on tempests and is never shaken."[9] But we know that that is the ideal. In actual practice our love is too often fickle, and our commitments too often flexible. When we look at all the deeds of power you have done for us, we can only praise your name. When, like the Virgin Mary, we look at the marvelous things you have done for us, we too can only shout for joy. But too often we are nearsighted, focusing only on ourselves, on our needs, on our whims. The light you have shared with us is a light meant to be directed outward. When it is only directed inward, we walk in the darkness our society or we ourselves have created. And so we stumble. Lord, lift up our eyes during this Holy Week. Open our eyes and our hearts so that we can see and respond to all the ways you demonstrated your saving love for us in your passion and death.

Though we were not there, keep us present to your great sacrifice in faith and in spirit, so that every day of our lives we can cry, "Blessed is the king who comes in the name of the Lord. Peace in heaven, and glory in the highest heaven." Amen.

Monday

Then he began to teach them that the Son of Man must undergo great suffering, and be rejected by the elders, the chief priests, and the scribes, and be killed, and after three days rise again. He said all this quite openly. And Peter took him aside and began to rebuke him. But turning and looking at his disciples, he rebuked Peter and said, "Get behind me, Satan! For you are setting your mind not on divine things but on human things."

Mark 8:31–33

Christ Jesus, loving Savior,

Because ours is an age of public relations and successful marketing, we can too readily understand, if not sympathize with, Peter. Accentuate the positive. Play up the good news of the gospel. People are sick and tired of hearing the negative. We deserve your words, Lord, just as much as Peter. "You are setting your mind not on divine things but on human things." You came into our lives not just to celebrate or make us feel good all of the time. You came to repair all the damage done by our selfishness and by our willfulness, by our baser choices and our meaner actions. You came to repair and restore the broken bond between our irresolute hearts and the divine heart that created us only to lavish upon us his very life and love. You, who were like us in all things except sin, took upon yourself all our sins, so that we might rise with you from both darkness and death. You are the lamb sacrificed for our sins. You are the healer and lover, who knows that all true love demands sacrifice and sometimes suffering. You are the healer and lover, who calls us now to open our hearts to your grace. You are the lamb, who calls us to live lovingly in both joy and sacrifice, in both suffering and celebration. Amen.

Tuesday

He called the crowd with his disciples, and said to them, "If any want to become my followers, let them deny themselves and take up their cross and follow me. For those who want to save their life will lose it, and those who lose their life for my sake, and for the sake of the gospel, will save it. For what will it profit them to gain the whole world and forfeit their life? Indeed, what can they give in return for their life? Those who are ashamed of me and of my words in this adulterous and sinful generation, of them the Son of Man will also be ashamed when he comes in the glory of his Father with the holy angels."

Mark 8:34–38

Christ Jesus, suffering Savior,

A woman's children and her husband gathered at her bedside during her final days. In her wasted form they saw what each doctor had seen; she had waited too long and the cancer now was too pervasive. She had reacted to the early signs and to the acute pains with fear and intense denial. This reaction is so human. We hope that if we ignore the illness, it will go away. We hope that if we delay the visit to the doctor and the diagnosis, the danger will not really exist. As long as the evil is denied, it is not real. But the opposite is more often true. In a desperate effort to cling to the life one knows, that person may lose that life. Both physically and spiritually, the person who wants to save his life must risk losing it. The sins and illness that threaten our life in you, Lord, never disappear when we ignore them or pretend that they don't really exist. Honestly facing whatever diminishes your life and image in us is a step toward life and health, not a surrender to the illness. Healing is painful, and every healing requires sacrifice. Our deepest healing, Lord, began with your suffering and sacrifice, with your passion and death. You came not to save us from suffering, but to teach us how to suffer. You came not to confirm and condemn our weak and sinful selves, but to heal and bring us life. Jesus, loving Savior, in your suffering and sacrifice are our healing. In you alone we are made healthy and whole. Amen.

Wednesday

They were on the road, going up to Jerusalem, and Jesus was walking ahead of them; they were amazed, and those who followed were afraid. He took the twelve aside again and began to tell them what was to happen to him, saying, "See, we are going up to Jerusalem, and the Son of Man will be handed over to the chief priests and the scribes, and they will condemn him to death; then they will hand him over to the Gentiles; they will mock him, and spit upon him, and flog him, and kill him; and after three days he will rise again."

Mark 10:32–34

Christ Jesus, our Strength,

How often do we hear someone say, "If I had only known how hard this was going to be, I never would have done it"? How often has this very thought crossed our own minds? Were we thinking of our job or of a project we had volunteered for? Raising our children through difficult years or phases? Living up to our word—or vow? Struggling to live up to what we say we believe? But you, Lord, saw so clearly and so vividly all that you would be subjected to and all that you would suffer through the days and hours of your terrible passion. "See, we are going up to Jerusalem, and the Son of Man will be handed over to the chief priests and the scribes, and they will condemn him to death; then they will hand him over to the Gentiles; they will mock him, and spit upon him, and flog him, and kill him...." And yet you went up to Jerusalem, up to the horrors of your suffering, up to your death. Why, Lord, why? Because you knew that when you were lifted up, you would draw all of us to yourself. Because you knew that there is no greater love than that of the person who lays down his life so that others may have life and may have it more abundantly. Because you knew that you would rise, and in your rising we too would be lifted up from pettiness and darkness, from death to eternal life. Lord, grace us with the strength and the courage to tackle those difficult things that our love and our responsibilities call us to. Because you have shown us the way. Because you are with us through even the most trying hours. Because your love is enduring and boundless. Because through your suffering we too can rise and know the joy of eternal life. Amen.

Holy Thursday

After he had washed their feet, had put on his robe, and had returned to the table, he said to them, "Do you know what I have done to you? You call me Teacher and Lord—and you are right, for that is what I am. So if I, your Lord and Teacher, have washed your feet, you also ought to wash one another's feet. For I have set you an example, that you also should do as I have done to you."

John 13:12–15

Christ Jesus, Servant and Savior,

Loving us so deeply that you humbled yourself, you chose to become fully human—like us in every frailty but sin. "Do you know what I have done for you?" Caring so deeply for us, you walked among us, healing us, restoring our sight, touching us to make us whole. "Do you know what I have done for you?" Seeing us stumbling and struggling, you spoke to us, guiding us and shining your light into the darkest corners of our fears and lives. "Do you know what I have done for you?" Watching our awkwardness and pride, you moved through your years on earth with such integrity and grace that we saw, in your example, the miracles and marvels of our human lives. "Do you know what I have done for you?" Knowing how close you were to your suffering and agonizing death, you rose from the table and gently, silently gave us a final example. Like a servant, humbly but with such love, you washed the feet of each of your disciples, of each of us. "Do you know what I have done for you?" Too often we do not realize what you have done for us and what you continue to do for us each day, each moment of our lives, Lord. "So if I, your Lord and Teacher, have washed your feet, you also ought to wash one another's feet. For I have set you an example, that you should also do as I have done to you." Amen.

Good Friday

After this, when Jesus knew that all was now finished, he said (in order to fulfill the scripture), "I am
thirsty." A jar full of sour wine was standing there. So
they put a sponge full of the wine on a branch of hys-
sop and held it to his mouth. When Jesus had
received the wine, he said, "It is finished." Then he
bowed his head and gave up his spirit.

John 19:28–30

Christ Jesus, Lamb of God,

Of all of the ways you could have reconciled us with
the Father, you agreed to the most agonizing and the most
humiliating. In the garden even the imagined horror of
your sacrifice made you sweat drops of blood. A word or
an act of your will would have cleansed us of our worst
and willful sins. But you wanted to show us the price of
our sins and the vastness of your love. "No one has greater
love than this, to lay down one's life for one's friends"
(John 15:13). Only the night before, at the breaking of
bread, you called us closer to you, not as servants, but as
friends. While the mere word of forgiveness from you
would have opened our lives to eternal life, how deeply
would we have been touched—we who are too often more
absorbed by our slightest whim than we are by your
boundless love. And so abandoned by most of your friends
and followers, you were mocked and stripped and
scourged. With criminals you were led through the streets
of Jerusalem as a common criminal. You were hung upon
a cross of execution, gasping for breath and slowly bleed-

ing to death. And you thought of us again and again in those terrible moments. And before your last breath, your last message to us was so simple: "I am thirsty." In your dying moments you spoke to us of your thirst for our love...for our return of the love that you lavish on us. "I am thirsty" for the commitment of your will to the will of the Father. Moments before your own heart was pierced with a spear, you spoke to us with your dying breaths: "I am thirsty" for your love, for a mind and heart open to my light and spirit. "I am thirsty"—that my suffering and death may not be in vain—for you, my friends, to say, "Lord, above all else, I thirst for you, in whom I am most fulfilled, most loved, and most fully alive." Amen.

Holy Saturday

And that is what the soldiers did. Meanwhile, standing near the cross of Jesus were his mother, and his mother's sister, Mary the wife of Clopas, and Mary Magdalene. When Jesus saw his mother and the disciple whom he loved standing beside her, he said to his mother, "Woman, here is your son." Then he said to the disciple, "Here is your mother." And from that hour the disciple took her into his own home.

John 19:25–27

Mary, Mother of Sorrows,

On our most hectic days, surrounded by noise and bedlam, we wish for quiet. But sometimes our most difficult days, like yours, are days of terrible loss and silence. Because of the great Sabbath, your son's body had been so hastily buried. The silence in the street was reflected in the silence in your house and in your heart. The horrors of the previous day could almost seem a nightmare, but the ache was too deep and the emptiness too vast. Thinking of a happier day, St. Luke had written: "Mary treasured all these words and pondered them in her heart" (Luke 2:19). How much more was that true on that silent Saturday, caught in stillness between wrenching agony and resurrection. And as you reflected on all these things, pondering them in your heart, was your faith strained—as our faith is sometimes strained? Was your hope tested, as our hope is sometimes tested? In his dying moments, the son you so dearly and deeply loved spoke to you, not as a reflection of his suffering and sorrows, but as a continuing image of hope for us. In his death and in his outstretched arms, he gave us a newer and richer life. In the son you gave birth to in Bethlehem we now have life and have it more abundantly. St. Paul could barely contain his joy: "It is no longer I who live, but it is Christ who lives in me" (Gal 2:20). Because in your son we live and move and have our truest being, your dying son reminded us that we have in you a model of hope and an enduring example of openness to his love, to his grace, and to the will of the Father. With John, we hear his words: "Here is your mother." Like John, we know that we have in your son, not death, but resurrection and eternal life. And in you, Mary, we have a heavenly and caring mother, concerned with our lives, our struggles, and with our resurrection in your son. Amen.

Easter Week

Easter Sunday

They found the stone rolled away from the tomb, but when they went in, they did not find the body. While they were perplexed about this, suddenly two men in dazzling clothes stood beside them. The women were terrified and bowed their faces to the ground, but the men said to them, "Why do you look for the living among the dead? He is not here, but has risen. Remember how he told you, while he was still in Galilee, that the Son of Man must be handed over to sinners, and be crucified, and on the third day rise again."

Luke 24:2–7

Christ Jesus, our Light and our Life,

The story was on every channel of the news. In the earthquake's final tremor, whole buildings collapsed, the roar of tons of concrete and steel drowning out the shrieks of the people being trapped. In the first day or two rescuers worked feverishly saving survivors trapped in the debris. When the days passed, with no sound of cries for help, the realists calculated that no one could still be alive without water or food or medical help. How foolish to expect any living person among the dead! Exhausted, teams of rescuers continued to excavate, pushing their hope and energy beyond human limits. And the miracle story emerged. As one huge slab of concrete was lifted, first the rescue dogs reacted, then the young woman was spotted, dehydrated, motionless, but alive. And the joy moved in waves through the rescuers and onlookers. A miracle! Nothing short of a miracle! Life emerges from a pit of wreckage and death. Because of you, our risen Lord, we can always look for and find life, even in death. Even greater than your resurrection is each rising from death in our lives. Our resurrection and enduring life in you is the great miracle. In you we have hope and can always rise out of our weakness and sins, out of suffering and discouragement, out of darkness and death. In you sorrow is always short-lived, and joy is enduring. You are the resurrection and the life, and in you both our lives and our joys are fulfilled. Amen.

Easter Monday

When he was at the table with them, he took bread, blessed and broke it, and gave it to them. Then their eyes were opened, and they recognized him; and he vanished from their sight. They said to each other, "Were not our hearts burning within us while he was talking to us on the road, while he was opening the scriptures to us?"

Luke 24:30–32

Christ Jesus, risen Lord,
Sitting at table with you, sharing a meal, your disciples recognized you. Such simple, shared things. In the blessing, breaking, and sharing of the bread—of your body—their eyes were opened and they recognized you, Lord. They recognized you in that simple and magnanimous sharing of your body and self. In our lives we see you most clearly in the simple, heartfelt sharings of each day. In our daily lives, the Father sees you in us most clearly in the simple, heartfelt sharing of our blessings and our very selves with those you have given us to love. In the simple sharing of our blessings and our selves, those around us see you, Lord, more surely, most resplendent, most truly risen and alive. Amen.

Easter Tuesday

Jesus said to her, "Woman, why are you weeping? Whom are you looking for?" Supposing him to be the gardener, she said to him, "Sir, if you have carried him away, tell me where you have laid him, and I will take him away." Jesus said to her, "Mary!" She turned and said to him in Hebrew, "Rabbouni!" (which means Teacher). Jesus said to her, "Do not hold on to me, because I have not yet ascended to the Father. But go to my brothers and say to them, 'I am ascending to my Father and your Father, to my God and your God.'"

John 20:15–17

Christ Jesus, risen Lord,

In the garden, thinking only of her heartache and grief, Mary did not at first recognize you. We can identify with her embarrassment so easily. Often we too have not recognized someone we should have known, should have recognized at once. Too often we have not recognized you, Lord, when we should have—in a friend's need for understanding, in a child's need for patience, in a spouse's need for affection or forgiveness. In the garden, you were there with Mary in a form and presence she did not expect or recognize. "Whom are you looking for?" Often our own vision is so clouded that we don't recognize you when you want to be seen. Too often our vision is blurred by our aversion to another's unpleasant illness, by our anger with our brother or friend, by our absorption in our every weakness or whim. Despite these distractions, your voice is still so clear: "Whom are you looking for?" For you, Lord. Simply you. Heal us of our blindness. Fill with grace our weakest moments, so that we can see you where you most want to be seen and love you when you most want to be loved. Amen.

Easter Wednesday

Jesus said to her, "Did I not tell you that if you believed, you would see the glory of God?" So they took away the stone. And Jesus looked upward and said, "Father, I thank you for having heard me. I knew that you always hear me, but I have said this for the sake of the crowd standing here, so that they may believe that you sent me." When he had said this, he cried with a loud voice, "Lazarus, come out!" The dead man came out, his hands and feet bound with strips of cloth, and his face wrapped in a cloth. Jesus said to them, "Unbind him, and let him go."

John 11:40–44

Christ Jesus, risen Lord,

You found yourself surrounded by men and women of limited faith. Mary complained, "If you had been here, my brother would not have died" (John 11:32). When you asked them to open Lazarus's tomb, Martha protested that the body had been lying there for four days already. Martha, Mary, and their friends did not even seem sure of what they were asking you to do. But you heard their words as clearly as you heard the longings of their hearts. For them you prayed, "Father, I thank you for having heard me. I knew that you always hear me...." Better than they themselves, you knew their needs and emptiness. Because you had both the power and the deep love, you called their brother and your friend back to life. "The dead man came out, his hands and feet bound with strips of cloth...." Lord, better than I myself, you know my needs and emptiness. Flawed as they are, they are my deepest prayer. I thank you for hearing me. I know that you always hear me. Tied hand and foot by my stubbornness and pettiness, you alone can untie me and let me go. I thank you for hearing me. Tied hand and foot by my prejudices and sloth, you alone can free me. I know that you always hear me. Because you have both the power and the deep love, you alone can call me out of darkness and death to sure and eternal life in you. Amen.

Easter Thursday

When it was evening on that day, the first day of the week, and the doors of the house where the disciples had met were locked for fear of the Jews, Jesus came and stood among them and said, "Peace be with you." After he said this, he showed them his hands and his side. Then the disciples rejoiced when they saw the Lord. Jesus said to them again, "Peace be with you. As the Father has sent me, so I send you." When he had said this, he breathed on them and said to them, "Receive the Holy Spirit. If you forgive the sins of any, they are forgiven them; if you retain the sins of any, they are retained."

John 20:19–23

Christ Jesus, Font of Life,

Terrified by the dangers outside and by the fears in their own hearts, your disciples tried to find security with locks and keys. They had seen some of the horrors inflicted on you. Their imaginations could too easily create images of what could happen to them. But as soon as you stood among them and said, "Peace be with you," they rejoiced. In you, in your presence, they knew both peace and joy. Without you, they knew only the paralysis of their fears. Because of our own fears and anxieties, we look for security as foolishly as did your first disciples. We count on our strength, on our plans and foresight, on our intelligence; we count on locks and keys. Only when we open our eyes and hearts, letting you who are always present to us, be truly present with us—only then can we know your peace and joy. The dangers will always exist; your presence is our strength and security. Your voice echoes through the ages and through our hearts, "Peace be with you." In you we know peace and joy, because you bring us a richer life in the Holy Spirit. With you we know peace and joy, because you forgive us our sins and failings each time we fail and confess our failings. Through you we know peace and joy, because you love us patiently and persistently with a love stronger than any danger and more invincible than death. Amen.

Easter Friday

A week later his disciples were again in the house, and Thomas was with them. Although the doors were shut, Jesus came and stood among them and said, "Peace be with you." Then he said to Thomas, "Put your finger here and see my hands. Reach out your hand and put it in my side. Do not doubt but believe." Thomas answered him, "My Lord and my God!" Jesus said to him, "Have you believed because you have seen me? Blessed are those who have not seen and yet have come to believe."

John 20:26–29

Christ Jesus, our Life and our Faith,

Just a week earlier, you paid the terrible price for our sins. Just a week earlier, you stretched out your arms on the cross so that we might know the depth of your love for us, so that we might be reconciled with both you and with the Father. But Thomas doubted what was too hard for him to believe—that you were truly the resurrection and the life. Peter had doubted, and in his doubt and fear he had denied you three times. To a man, your apostles had doubted you, fleeing through the darkened garden in their fear. Most astounding is not our doubts, but your continuing faith in us. The sacrifice on Calvary was consummated because of your continuing love for us, because of your continuing faith in us, even when you see such doubt or indifference in us. What have you seen in us to justify your faith and love for us? Your words are our comfort: "Blessed are those who have not seen and yet have come to believe." Lord, like Thomas, we have seen the signs of your faith in us. Like him, we have felt the depth of your love for us. Touch our hearts and our souls with your grace, so that we may not be unbelieving, but believing. Touch our hearts and our souls with your grace, so that, like Thomas, we may say with faith and love: "My lord and my God!" Amen.

Easter Saturday

Later he appeared to the eleven themselves as they were sitting at the table; and he upbraided them for their lack of faith and stubbornness, because they had not believed those who saw him after he had risen. And he said to them, "Go into all the world and proclaim the good news to the whole creation. The one who believes and is baptized will be saved; but the one who does not believe will be condemned."

Mark 16:14–16

Christ Jesus, our Resurrection and our Life,

Moses complained that he could not speak well. Jonah looked for a quick escape when the Lord called. The rich young man turned and walked sadly away from you. And what is our response when you tell us: "Go into all the world and proclaim the good news to the whole creation"? Do we confess our fear—or even reluctance? Do we acknowledge that our words and our actions are often at odds? Do we admit how feeble an example we sometimes set in our daily actions? Lord, you know our frailties as surely as you knew the limitations of Moses or Jonah or Peter or Thomas or John. The light that shines to light the world is not our weakness, but your grace in us. The light that shone in the young woman in Nazareth was your very life in her. You ask of us what you asked of Mary—faith and assent. You ask of us what you asked of Moses or Jonah or Peter or Paul—faith and openness to all the richness of your living grace. And when we believe and let your grace transform our lives, then we can say with Mary: "My soul magnifies the Lord, and my spirit rejoices in God, my Savior, for he has looked with favor on the lowliness of his servant" (Luke 1:46–48). Amen.

Notes

1. http://outofthedesert.wordpress.com/2008/09/29/mantra-monday-the-glory-of-god-is-man-fully-alive/.

2. Barry J. Trick, *Sparks from the Anvil* (Bogotá, Colombia: Incarnate Words, 2007), 26.

3. Thomas McNally, CSC, and William G. Storey, *Day by Day* (Notre Dame, IN: Ave Maria Press, 2004), 15.

4. Cleanth Brooks, John T. Purser, and Robert Penn Warren, editors, *An Approach to Literature*, fourth edition (New York: Appleton-Century-Crofts, 1964), 816.

5. Thomas McNally, CSC, and William G. Storey, *Day by Day* (Notre Dame, IN: Ave Maria Press, 2004), 15.

6. Richard DeLillio, OSFS, editor, *A Spoonful of Honey* (Wilmington, DE: Oblate Development Office), 34.

7. William Shakespeare, *The Tragedy of Hamlet, Prince of Denmark*, ed. Barbara A. Mowat and Paul Werstine (New York: Washington Square Press, Folger Shakespeare Library, 1992), 169.

8. Carl E. Bain, Jerome Beaty, and J. Paul Hunter, editors, *The Norton Introduction to Literature*, second edition (New York: W. W. Norton and Company, 1977), 615.

9. William Shakespeare, *The Complete Works of William Shakespeare*, ed. George Lyman Kittredge (New York: Ginn and Company, 1936), 1512.